NOT IF,
WHEN

NOT IF, WHEN

LYME DISEASE IN VERSE
GAIL TIERNEY

SHE WRITES PRESS

Published 20202
Printed in the United States of America
ISBN: 978-1-63152-735-7 pbk
ISBN: 978-1-63152-736-4 ebk
Library of Congress Control Number: 2020905901

For information, address:
She Writes Press
1569 Solano Ave #546
Berkeley, CA 94707

Illustrations by Kate Burke
Interior design by Tabitha Lahr

She Writes Press is a division of SparkPoint Studio, LLC.

Contents

nine months. 1

mud pot thoughts. 2

during the time of not knowing. 3

scraped clean. 4

parasitic debut. 5

honey badgers don't give a shit. 6

like a virgin. 7

Siri came for me in the nighttime 8

thanks, man. 9

field notes 10

don't read this one to your aunt with the pink ribbon 11

poor connection; mailbox full 12

for everyday. 13

confused in the middle of a crosswalk 14

there's a reason for florists 16

from a floor in Nicaragua 17

jetlag 19

on pops's response to poops 20

zoinks, bugman 21

yelling is fun 22

narcissism 23

CDC, look @ me. 24

bad mood 25

woof 26

teeth-marked tongue 27

yep, I'm looking for attention—from doctors 28

control issues 29

hello, my name is 30

blown kisses 31

a little coitus never hoitus. 32

stick of doom, you say? 33

stop rewind >> play. 34
new growth 36
bloodshed 37
I am frustration hear me roar 38
palpitation. 39
Ha! 40
become like Liam Neeson. 41
slow turn towards the sky. 42
seaweed baths are a holy experience 44
no one can resist Mel's brownies 46
no longer confined, but redefined 48
for rock bottom 49
remember, Simba 50
"bite me" isn't my go-to taunt. 51
Chlorella, Chlorella Deville. 52
the spiritual practice of .53
Did you drink the hippie-dippie jungle juice
    or something?. 54
An Ode to Magma Shoulders 55
not today, Satan. 56
walking alongside others 57
sometimes I respond to something someone said
    after they leave 59
the greatest insight 60
gesundheit. 61
mandala 62
thanks, mom 63
one of the first things I wrote down 64
REI made a solid point on Black Friday. 66
remember your roots, and let them root for you 67
to those of you who are sick 69
to the tick 70
I just got Cindy Lou Who'ed. 71
my hope for you 72

sometimes random suffering points to
   not-so-random suffering 73

so fresh so clean 75

occupied 76

hiker praise 77

riddle me this 78

press conference 79

sick of tears and skippin' the beers 80

British buddy 81

reframe 82

a pox on the rutabaga! 83

a sidewalk somewhere 84

what if 85

apothecary banter 86

shots on shots 87

take a break 88

you lead, I'll follow 90

txts from last night 91

is it still a secret in a published book? 92

my face amongst the trees 93

ran fresh outta words 94

splish-splash 95

Tinder profile 96

I do 97

road trip! where to? 99

accessible 100

Welp 101

Chekhovian delight 102

repetition 104

banana peel 105

Apostles of Beauty 106

towards the end of a book, it's good to paraphrase 108

all for now 109

"Wait, so a doctor said it's chronic,
and I'll have to think about it for the rest of my life . . ."
But <u>you</u> can say it's a little resistant,
but you get to begin a lifelong odyssey in the
persistent pursuit of health
through spa days, gentleness, and nights
looking up at the heavens.

That isn't to say that the words of the medical
community won't both hurt and heal you.
Or that you won't be angry and tired of
fighting your insides.

But there <u>will</u> be beauty along this journey,
and you are not alone.

Over 300,000 people are infected with Lyme disease in the USA each year, but if you don't take antibiotics within the first six weeks of the bug bite (which many people don't detect), there is nothing that the traditional Western medical community will do for you. The CDC does not recognize Chronic Lyme.

Some doctors recognize that patients have continued symptoms after taking a course of antibiotics, but they attribute them to some other condition. Many people have been buried in a pile of untrue medical labels and harsh pharmaceutical prescriptions because of those politics. It is time we call Chronic Lyme what it is and give patients the support they deserve.

If you are reading this book, you may be directly impacted by Chronic Lyme disease. You may have it. A family member may be disappearing before your eyes. There may be a friend or lover who has entered your life and whispered the words in shame. I wrote these poems with a very specific audience in mind—those patients who are running out of patience or struggling to stay afloat amidst the daunting challenge of healing. They are a love letter to you. But that's not to say that others cannot find the content insightful.

This is a glimpse of a brain undergoing trauma. Some might call it autobiographical poetry. Or a published diary. Or a snorkel dive into a different perspective. Perhaps you'll experience the calming effect of watching another life swim by, moving and breathing, going about its business.

These poems are not organized. They were written for me, for us, and for anyone else who cares to be involved. They travel through personal pain and emotional maturation. I have left them in their original form—in the order that they spilled out of me in a torrent. They are fragmented recalls and futile attempts at writing the trauma into my narrative.

I have since learned that trauma stops time. It deactivates the left, analytical and chronologically inclined side of the brain. In the months after my lowest health points, it was entirely common to freeze, collapse, and face an inability to convey the horror of my story in words. Therefore, you will find no chapters, subcategories, or satisfying schemas. That's not the text that was written into my body, so it is not the text I've captured on the page. I have tried not to overedit the bad and the ugly pieces out. If there's teen angst oozing out of a poem, well, that happens some days. It can be very difficult to stay lifted, and many are not as privileged and lucky as I am with the care that they access.

You will see, however, that a new voice emerges as the pages turn. This is where the hope lies. Mixed into the clearly unstable, imbalanced chemistry of my reality, there are mantras, mystical encounters, and resilience beyond my imagination. You, too, contain the powerful potential to heal yourself or other living beings.

I didn't read everything out there on Lyme disease to write this book. It is not intended to offer medical insight or scholarly commentary (although it's about time our lived experiences gain validity as scholarly sources). This is a snapshot of one young woman's inner life at a particular moment in history—a moment when her treatments were all based on educated guesses. By purchasing this book, you've participated in destigmatizing a disease that affects millions of people worldwide. Thank you.

It may be helpful for you to approach this story with a brief timeline in mind. Here is a loose framework of the contributing circumstances in my life:

2012 I worked at a summer camp where I likely contracted Lyme disease. It is impossible to know decisively when the infection occurred, but in retrospect, I experienced sleep paralysis, vivid dreams, and a few other characteristic symptoms. I assumed these were stress responses to my new responsibilities and surroundings.

2012– As my college years passed, I developed a mysterious dairy "allergy."

2016 I noticed a particular sensitivity to alcohol but attributed it to a family history of alcoholism. I also had bouts of terror and rage that seemed unconnected to anything in my life. In each instance, I dealt with the immediate inconvenience and kept moving with my busy, daily rhythms.

2017   I took a job at a social justice nonprofit in Nicaragua. Within a few months, I was incredibly ill with fevers, brain fog, pain, diarrhea, impaired eyesight, and other symptoms. I visited local clinics and a national hospital, trying to find the root cause. As the symptoms of the illness began to affect major organs such as my heart as well as my respiratory and digestive systems, I was gripped with fear for my life and returned to the United States.

    I spent a few months in a cycle of blood work, stool tests, CAT scans, EKGs, referrals, an endoscopy, infectious disease specialists, and questions about whether I may be pregnant or mentally unsound.

    Later that year, I made my way to an integrative health practice where I learned that I had become host to a smorgasbord of parasites during my travels and that the stress to my body had caused a flare-up of the underlying Lyme infection.

2018   I spent the tail end of 2017 and the beginning of 2018 volunteering in Northern Ireland. I shipped boxes of antibiotics and supplements through customs, routinely visited the bathroom for panic attacks and other expressions of Herxheimer reactions, and relied heavily on the care of my community to get well. All of the poems in this collection were written during the turbulent, enriching months of that volunteer position.

Here's to naming the things you don't want to re-member
for the sake of putting them down and moving forward
pasito a pasito
wee step after wee step

I didn't want to read books
I don't think I would've read this book

I didn't want to introduce myself as the illness
especially when it felt like my most defining trait

let people have their silence
unless you're really close
and then ask compassionate questions
because they want you to know
they just might not know how to let you in

I know for a fact that most people could fill an entire book with the years of goose-hunting a Lyme-literate practitioner.

I am so sorry.

You're not crazy. You're a motherfucking warrior.

nine months

the ticks of a clock
or a forest
as the seasons shift

just enough to incubate a life
or for a previously captive Irishman to reenter the darkness
and for a young woman to trust that she's not going to die
        swallow her disappointment
and start writing about the joys of her stepping stones
as she splashed through and to her wellspring

mud pot thoughts

I've felt ugly for months
but sometimes
I get out of the apartment
and walk down the street
mentally screaming

I've been pissing bright orange
and shitting gold flakes
for the better part of a year
BOW DOWN, PEASANTS

during the time of not knowing

I don't know how many nights I went to sleep
unsure if I would wake up

so when my family asked
that I sleep in another room
I understood

I didn't want to give them the plague

but I sobbed
because I was willing to risk my sister's health
so that I wouldn't die alone

scraped clean

I envied the cantaloupe
up against a spork

a few clean scrapes
and you can gut the whole rind

I didn't want to crawl out of my skin
I wanted to incinerate it
blast dynamite
rip, power-wash, and wring

I wanted my body back

& this was fucking war.

parasitic debut

A worm came out of my nose during a business meeting
and I laughed
so another one came out of my ear

but then
I courageously watched a documentary
with a soundtrack of doom
and there was an animation where spirochetes
burrowed
into the cartoon's brain, intestines, liver, heart, lungs . . .
and sleep was out of the question

I remember clawing into my own flesh
with fingernails
tweezers
my mother's gentle hands

until I cried,
"Stop. We're hurting me, not them."

honey badgers don't give a shit

nobody else knows
nobody else will ever know
nobody else can fight for you
nobody else can see the fight

so cover your wall with sticky notes saying:
You don't want to die.
You're not going to die.
You can do this.
You are so strong.

Blast Ke$ha or Sia at all times
and whisper, "You're doing so well"
the illness may be invisible, but you know what's not?
the confidence you choose every damn day
wear it like your favorite worn-in tee

like a virgin

Lyme aside
I've always been on the fence about babies
someone dear called them potatoes
another aliens
and I can't shake the heebie-jeebies

so I never understood the mania
around firsts

that is until
I celebrated milestones of my own

the first
        period
                bowl of cereal
                        bike ride to the doctor's office

healing is like retrieving tiny grains of dirt from a semi-closed
wound
swab the alcohol and it stings
break skin and it tingles
dig deeper and deeper and bleed and bite your lip
and you'll have a pretty good chance of ~~pokemoning~~ catching
them all

Siri came for me in the nighttime

on my birthday
I was in an airport
with my older sister
and I thought I'd pass out
from all of the iPhones, iPads, MacBooks

I didn't want to be the crazy woman
seeing force fields and light-saber wielding trolls
where others saw amusements to pass the time

I tried to ask a few people to keep those devices away
but I quickly saw
they wouldn't

thinking you may vomit from looking at a GPS
is not normal
and people make accommodations for the abnormal
to an extent

the rest of the gap is left for you to close

thanks, man

in a grocery store
I mentioned to my cousin,
"If I ever get better, I'll eat that."
                              When!
                              He interrupted,
"Not if, when."

field notes

I don't use words like "chronic"
or "*my* disease"

the mind is a powerful thing

don't read this one to your aunt with the pink ribbon

this won't win popularity points
but I've envied people with cancer

not for their fight
which I cannot imagine

but for the response of the masses

What's the magic password?
Cancer.
Violà!
a fridge full of food, a secret Facebook page, an army of tightly
gripping hands and stoic shoulders to sponge up tears

Lyme opens doors to
"Are you sure?"
"That's not so bad"
"My friend had that and she's fine"
or worse yet
"That's not real"
"You're imagining things"
there is no vaccine, acknowledged treatment, or cure

poor connection; mailbox full

She tried to tell me for years
sunrise
over a bowl of honey o's
when running became difficult
and I blamed my blameless spirit
sunset
no time
not when there's degrees to be gotten
and money to be holed away like acorns for a long, cold nap
She told me with bile rising to my throat
burning the truth like a cow's hide branding
not today
with internships and scholarships and all the ships that keep
our feet firmly on land
watching the skin on our hands age while we wonder if we'll
ever go on an expedition of our own
days to weeks to months to years
I'm sorry, beautiful one.
you were sick. you are sick.
you deserve to be well.
please tell me what you need
I'm listening
and I promise to listen for every day that I breathe
healthy
like the ageless rocks and moss and sand
who deserve it maybe more

for everyday

You got this little body.
You got this, little body.

confused in the middle of a crosswalk

I started to have many thoughts that began with
"If I were healthy"

If I were healthy, I'd stop the cab here and grab that one grocery
If I were healthy, I'd do something useful

healthy people reach for pills
because they will make it better
numb the pain
hurry up the healing

But each new medication
left me more raw than before

it would be an inexcusable understatement to say
it has to get worse before it gets better

the first sip of that tincture knocked me to the floor
convulsing
seizing in the throws of a panic attack

the first round of that antibiotic
fogged my brain until I didn't know my name
until walking was an exertion that I rationed

when a herx is waiting at the end of a swallow
you begin to fear medications
or, more accurately, the unknown that comes with them

there were many times when I wanted to be hospitalized
so a nurse could lie to me
explain exactly how I would respond
open my mouth for me and force the remedy down

so that I wouldn't be doing it to myself

there's a reason for florists

please don't photograph my face
not yet
wait until the darkness lifts from my retinas

the shadow of your pain completely eclipsed

what I do wish I could photograph
were the stems and bouquets and arrangements
carefully swaddled in my forearms
like the children I may never have

bustled through the revolving door
and welcomed into that empty apartment
fraaaands!

thanks for your colorful calm
for holding space when I've cried
and kissing my runny nose with scents sweeter than the
Ghirardelli factory
I should've photographed you all

your tiny tribes could probably fill a wall
instead, I've sewn you into my rib cage
my arteries
my pancreas, kneecaps, and spleen

it may take a village to raise a child
but for this, it takes a garden
handpicked.

from a floor in Nicaragua

It hurts
lying in stillness, but my chest is heaving with the movement of
my heart
I don't want to throb for anyone
because honestly, it's not pleasant
my stomach inflated like a turkey bred for slaughter
malnourished, pumped with air while barbed wire ribs
pronounce themselves louder than ever
está bien
don't worry about me
water drowns the pain momentarily
just long enough to stagger to the bathroom
until the floor calls once again and the pain sets down deeper
in my womb now, extending into my groin and my inner thigh
it hurts
but I don't want you to see me cry
so into the bathroom I go
meeting the gaze of the globes in my forehead
and shattering
because the light is dimmer
a flicker in the home of a supernova
you can do this
one step at a time
a few kilometers in the heat
suero suero suero and a laugh to help the heart pangs
climb a mountain in a sopping wet dress
because cognition failed on that one
but the mosquitoes leave me be for now
they can see it's not a good day
Are you okay?

No. Let's hike that trail anyway
laying supine next to the parakeet hovels
contemplating the line between adventure and crazy
doubting there is one
swinging a machete to slice a slim branch clean off
just like that it's gone
like me
and only dead fish go with the flow
so I can get my life together in the bathrooms and then climb
mountains
until I can't
       and then what
              I'm not a machine
take a step back
even if it's fun right here
it can be very fun to self-destruct

jetlag

When I first arrived in Belfast,
my host parents told me that I looked shattered

THE FUCK?!

I've been putting pieces together like a madwoman, hop off my
ovaries!

. . . it means tired

when you start to dip your toes into the pool of normalcy
you may want to backpedal
and point to where you're coming from

on paps's response to poops

I'll never forget
my father's face
after the first time I pooped my pants

I was laughing

and he was not

I laughed so hard
I did it again

but his eyes were full of sorrow
and red-hot fear

zoinks, bugman

there have been bugs under my skin for months
        only they're not really there
I thought they were eating my brain
or crawling down my throat
        but they were actually signaling in their own language

right when you start to wrap your non-eaten brain
around that fact

the inevitable will happen

a tiny critter will traipse across your calf
with confidence in the shortest path

the one he has chosen

you won't brush him away
after all, he's imaginary

warning: you may go through the roof
or slanty if you're leaning
point is: you will get major air
like a cat making acquaintance with a cucumber

that reintroduction to
a natural occurrence
of the wayward bug
is not something I can prepare you for

yelling is fun

on a road trip with friends
we pulled the car over
and I stood at the rim of a mountain

and screamed something like
"You picked the wrong woman to fuck with!!!"

Very dramatic
felt a bit performative
5/5 would recommend

double-dog dare you because it's the truth. You're a warrior.
You know it (and now, so do all of the dandelions from here
to Timbuktu).

narcissism

I ended up in the Cubs stadium
at a point when I was a hilariously hot mess

fresh air was making me hiccup uncontrollably
and gusts of wind would make me keel over

so I imagined that the roars of boozy cheering
were applause directly aimed at me

and I smugly sat in eerie silence
narcissistically accepting their congratulatory whoops

CDC, look @ me

when I looked into the doctors' eyes
I knew that they couldn't help
that they wouldn't lose sleep over my unanswered case

they were handing me Band-Aids
and I wanted a cure

so I kept clawing my way
because that's all there is to do
when you're too young to die
and you have a sinking suspicion that antidepressants
aren't the right diagnosis

bad mood

don't let anyone tell you
that your method of healing
is unnatural
or not enough
or excessive

take the time to wallow
spend all your money on organic food
refuse to speak to anyone for a day
do what you have to do to survive

it's actually not your responsibility to educate others
on the best ways to help you

woof

I remember reading on Doctor Google
about a woman who couldn't move for weeks
because the weight of what was being lifted
was too heavy

and thought
phew
that sucks

and climbed in bed for a few months

teeth-marked tongue

every time I put on clothes and got outside
was a tiny victory
so when someone I loved wanted more from me
like an explanation of how it felt
or a day of activities like walking down the street and touring
a museum

I silently yelled,
"I've already done so much! I'm here! You could've come and
laid in bed and made me laugh, but you didn't. I packed up my
medicines and got my toxin-filled ass on public transportation
to show you how much I care!"

yep, I'm looking for attention—from doctors

looking back at the years
where the sickness was duller
but present
is haunting

I remember a trip to the beach
where I couldn't get comfortable
so I did a headstand
to give my blood a big flush
like the two droplet option in a gas station
and my uncle said,
"someone wants us to look at her"

my cousin said something in my defense
but I can't remember what it was

I got up and sprinted in the opposite direction

control issues

I want to erase the pictures from half a decade
because I can see it

the strangeness in my eyes
the distress in my smile

I don't think anyone else can,
but I can see it

and I'd rather erase them
than show the world a person I no longer want to be

hello, my name is

first impressions when you're sick
suck

because we're visual, intuitive creatures
and people will think that you are angry, uninterested, closed
off, defensive, rude, unkind, unkempt, unprofessional, and ugly

and you know what, sometimes you are

but you can't wait to go on living until you have it together
where would you go?

you need to keep attempting the things you want to do
even if you fail
even if people are disappointed with your work ethic

because you're working so much harder than a healthy person
but they don't need to know
keep that powerful little secret

blown kisses

I won't promise much
because my story is different than yours
and chronic illness isn't usually the protagonist in a happy ending

but I will promise this:
it slows down

not every step you take will feel like the earth is crumbling
beneath you
not every bite of food will paralyze with fear
eventually
gradually
subtly
there will be space in your brain for things other than your
mortality

if I could
I'd give this to you for Christmas
in a neat little package

a little coitus never hoitus

lots of things have helped me get better
but one worth mentioning is
orgasms

they haven't involved anyone else
I've often felt too weak or traumatized or germaphobic for that

and maybe it's too soon for you
maybe the idea of sex makes you roll your eyes and think, "how
do you have energy for that?" and "if anyone tries to touch me,
I will amputate on the spot"

valid

oh so valid

give the calendar a few turns and then get back on the bike or
couch or fingers or dick

you deserve to feel pleasure again

stick of doom, you say?

for months and months
I was pretending to be a human

doom on a stick
disguised as a young woman

and that was so exhausting
that I found it hilarious

I'd invite you, too, to laugh
doom on a stick is absurd
doom on a stick is not socially appropriate
doom on a stick probably can't remember the word "socially
appropriate" because it's too busy being doom on a stick and
clearing toxins

hysterical

stop rewind >> play

I was vacuuming a floor today
when I burst into tears

sometimes the images pop into my eyes
impossible to ignore until they're
seen felt released

this time
it was the blood-crusted sheets that clung to my skin
the blood not mine
the bed not mine
the choice not mine what was injected into that IV

it was my pops a dops
sitting across from my elevated hospital bed
as I confessed,
"I thought I was going to die, Dad."
"That's not good, Gaily."

I imagined walking into the medical practice
stepping through the door from Clybourn Street
blinking away sunbeams
to find a tunnel of practitioners in a standing ovation
clapping for me
cheering for the astounding progress I'd made

I was lying in bed today
when I burst into tears

a lever released and my head was raised for me
but it wasn't a hospital bed
it was a massage table
and the seaweed dripped from my hair
with the same velocity
as the salt water from my eye sockets

new growth

I cut my hair because I wanted to shed the dead fibers

they have mopped my cheeks of so many tears
turned jet-black as a cry for attention

I was sick of the best view being from behind
I wanted to see my beauty, strength, and resilience head-on
with a better view than anyone who is watching me walk away

this illness may be invisible
and it does not make my hair fall out
so I am choosing to wear it differently

because I am differently

bloodshed

it helps to watch myself cry
looking in a mirror watching the tears explode out of my tear
ducts and shake my little frame
because it's the one time it's not invisible
I see them
I see the tears
they're proof when the doctors and the nonchalant askers about
"lymes" and the new friends cannot know
I see them and they drip to the floor or the crease of my elbow
where the IV bruises have faded
I am bleeding salt water
I've been bleeding for over a year now

I am frustration hear me roar

it isn't fair
how come he is barred from leaving his country
unable to cross these imaginary lines we call borders
because of the decade and some change that he spent in a
torturous inhumane block of concrete
he wants to be a ski instructor in the alps
but he can't do that.
instead he serves people poison in a dark, moldy room
and walks alongside the "peace" walls with gawking tourists
when he was brainwashed as a child
conditioned to the point that he saw targets rather than humans

meanwhile I'm walking calmly onto planes
traveling all over the globe
tracking mud full of microorganisms that are probably killing
whole food chains
when I might be a fucking contagion

it's so goddamn heavy
the weight of these things you didn't ask to host in the first place

palpitation

just this once I thought I'd be able to see it
my heart pounding clawing its way out of my chest
but why would that be possible
it will always be invisible

Ha!

today
today is my lucky day
today I happened to be wearing a raincoat
so the pitter-patter of tears
rolled down a surface that was resistant

for once

become like Liam Neeson

there is nowhere to hide
not abroad
in another country
or with a new name or personality or wardrobe

you can't run from the disease that is inside you
fracturing you apart
pulling at the pieces of you that are patient kind and content
and infecting them with fear

I have lain in fetal position in different cities countries and dwell-
ings over the past few years
some with plumbing
others with cockroaches
I have clutched more than one knife between my fingertips

buzzing with false confidence
that I could slice wound or kill the source of my goose bumps

but that was an artificial reality
instead
in this head
I am paralyzed
by the bacteria which have burrowed their roots into my innards

you, little miss, are going to have to be fucking brave

slow turn towards the sky

I told the doctor that I was starting to feel dependent on
antibiotics
afraid of what would happen when I stopped taking them
of what would happen to me

so she told me to do some body affirmation journaling

and I chopped off all my hair
felt really sexy

started to say a mantra on the toilet
rocking and crying
as you do

quite often actually

I can do this
you can do this
you are strong enough
I am strong enough
look how far you've come
you're doing so well
you are getting so well
I can do this
we can do this we can do this

. . . where did the *we* come from?

maybe God is listening and caring and investing time in each of
Her trembling daughters

GAIL TIERNEY   43

seaweed baths are a
holy experience

looking at my reflection in the tinted glass
as people walk by outdoors
and I soak up the nutrients from the sea
the largest wellspring

seen by many as the largest toilet

but, for this hour, I'm not thinking of the floating turd of rubbish
called a gyre

for this hour
I will gently brush my skin with the soft exfoliating mitt
my inner thighs
the gaps between my toes
I'll float weightlessly

and laugh with the owner of the spa
when she drives me home because I'm the only customer and
it's raining outside

the friendships that form between women and their aestheticians
are holy
the woman who plucks your eyebrows
waxes your pubic hairs
rubs your tired, used muscles
so much vulnerability and storytelling and love

thank you to all of the women who have touched, cared for, pampered, and healed our bodies
I hope someone has kissed your cheek and sent you flowers just because

no one can resist Mel's brownies

it smelled so good
and everyone else was eating it
everyone else gets to eat it
so I took a bite
and it tasted so good
and my jawbone came unhinged
unable to shovel fast enough
like Pac-Man in a field full of chocolate chip muffins
because doctors' orders can't touch me now

I'm so sorry
I rock and sob it to my sinews my tissues my bones

I'm so sorry
from the bathroom stall

where I'm reminded that I'm not normal
that I'm sick

be patient, I cry
but I don't remember what caramel tastes like
I don't remember what it's like to savor a dessert without
inhaling it before I can think twice
because I'm guilty, cheating, not helping myself

help yourself
what a hilariously aggressive thing to tell someone

I'm no superhero
it was right there

I ate myself into this brain fog
I ate myself backwards
I'll eat myself into the ground because I don't know how to let
someone hold this anger, impatience, childishness

no longer confined, but redefined

somehow
I've stopped falling to my knees in gratitude for each step, breath,
morning I get out of bed
somehow
I'm moving
wondering how to make sense of this massive event and let it
inform my life
somehow
I'm thinking of when I may drink red wine again
somehow, I don't know how
which brings me to my knees in gratitude

for rock bottom

you don't want to die
tell it to yourself even when it feels like a lie
say it over and over and over again

tell someone that you're thinking it
say it out loud

get someone to check on you
surround yourself with love
have them remind you how much your life affects other people,
systems, and communities

say it until you believe it
I don't want to die
there is so much to live for
even if the present is excruciatingly undesirable

remember, Simba

healed and held
loved and lifted

you got this, little body

"bite me" isn't my go-to taunt

literally though . . .
did it bite me in my butt crack
or between my labia
or in the dent on my skull beneath all my wavy hair
where the fuck was that little fuck
and how didn't I see it?!

can I add a disclaimer to my future partners:
you must love playing outside
with a strong willingness to check my butt crack
between my labia
the dent on my skull beneath my wavy hair
because I will not go through this bullshit ever again

Chlorella, Chlorella Deville

I don't know the names of the co-infections
or the parasites or the Lyme shenanigans
makes it harder to slaughter them if they're endeared li'l named
dears running around the green fields of my chest cavity
Nope. I never asked.
I do know the names of the medicines. Some of them have
nicknames.
Signs of affection for helping me so much.
Sometimes, I cup them in my palm and mutter,
"Be kind to me."
"I know you're a wrecking ball—do the good work, but please
leave me standing."
For example, the turmeric capsules have a name that sounds
like *CurCur*
before I swallow, I often give a little wiggle and sing,
"I'm in love with the CurCur!"

the spiritual practice of . . .

There's this thing called meditation
You may want to give it a try
it helps me grab the pain by the shoulders
give it a good shake and then a massage

"When you meet the Buddha, shoot the Buddha,"
an acting teacher once said

the meditation guide's name is Andy, and he lives in my earbuds
Boyfriend Andy, I fucking love you.
You're helping me relax my way towards healing

Some people like walking meditation
or cleaning meditation
May I recommend the finest spiritual practice of all—
crying meditation

That's right. You heard it here, folks. Get a good rock going and
let out years of tears.
The ones your cells were wailing before you could hear.

Did you drink the hippie-dippie jungle juice or something?

in Galway, with a pal, I wanted to cut loose
we went to a club
or, more accurately, I went to the bathroom of the club and had
a panic attack
my body looks whole
but there are holes in my energetic body
the outer one
the one you know exists because of Michelangelo but probably
don't talk about because that's weird until there's holes in that
protective, vital bubble
and all of the lust, shame, insecurities, and moves busted with
abandon have no shield to ricochet
they seep right into your solar plexus
little daggers, taking and depleting
making your breaths shallow and gasping

Lawd Jesus, can someone hand me some duct tape?

An Ode to Magma Shoulders

you're killin' me, guys
OUCH
relief occasionally after a scorching shower or a lather of magnesium
absorbing with the sting of 17 baby jellyfishes

when I get all cracked out on hulk antibiotic energy
you burn
when I'm hungry or tired or bored
you burn
when I listen to some great music or check myself out in a mirror
you burn

Could you be a little more original?

not today, Satan

"This won't be a big deal in the grand scheme of things."

"You need to look at the larger picture."

"You're not pulling your weight."

"If you get sick, you need to tell someone."

"It's unacceptable to disappear for 20 minutes without telling me."

"You're not keeping up."

Ignore them and go take a nap because you deserve it.

walking alongside others

I guess I'll be healing from something all the time from now on
we all are, really
detoxing the chemical cloud we walked through
or burning off the flu
or snotting out a bug
all the more reason to be gentle with myself
take it easy, zeezee

this perspective makes it easier to relate to others who are
healing from all kinds of things
because to some extent healing is healing
once you get that ball rolling
it's all like "hoist the sails, boys! It's healing timeee!"

so this morning I was talking to a boy whose dad died
about 6 months ago
and I saw the raw quivers of his chest
the crocodile tears welling at the bottom of his eyeballs
threatening to spill over
and I asked him what makes him happy to be alive
        there was a millisecond where I felt like an insensitive dick
because we get to live for whatever reason

but then, his spine reached for the sky with a lightness as he
smiled the word
"farming"

boy, do I understand that boy
he wants to heal the earth
he wants to work the earth

he wants to feed his body
he wants to feed other bodies

we talked about industrial farms and sustainable diets with meat
did I mention that he was 11?
what a day

a truly great day for the parish

sometimes I respond to something someone said after they leave

Please don't say to someone with chronic illness:

"When I'm sick, I just want to be at home, you know? Like with my mom making me soup."

Yeah, well, duh. Everyone wants that. Life doesn't stop for that possibility.

the greatest insight

What do you call a bee who's having a bad hair day?

A frisbee.

. . . that one has nothing to do with anything, but jokes are
important.

gesundheit

I've heard a lot of people sneeze in my life
it's a thing that people do semi-regularly
and I've always found it funny for the response to be "bless you"
and I've heard people theorize about a time when the common
cold could kill ya, so those blessings were necessary
but I always want to add a "child" to the end
so everyone is just walking around going, "bless you, child" in
nonchalant tones

but, I shit you not, here's the kicker:
I think every body part has been involved in this battle in some
way or another
symptoms I can't even remember because I wanted to let them
pass through without documentation
migrant status for sureee
vibrating vision
a drum line heartbeat
a spleen that liked to scream
knees, elbows, wrists, thumbs, ankles, neck, you get the picture
with pop rocks inside
I found myself instinctively laying my hands on the loudest
screamer
and silently blessing it
I'll be damned—it worked

mandala

during the period of not knowing
when I was calling it a mystery plague

I drew myself a bath
and slowly lowered my tired bones into the hot water
my belly was bloated
because it was a packed house in there at the time

and blood started rushing to my core
it formed a beautiful mandala
a truly gorgeous design

and I sensed that it was gathering, sweeping, and purifying my blood

I dripped all the way down the hallway
with crazed eyes to tell my parents, "You're never going to
believe what just happened! It's like an adult coloring book on
my abdomen!"
but the design had already vanished

sometimes, when I lose trust in my body
that it knows what it's doing
that nothing else is hiding
I think of that bath
before any doctors took me seriously
before any medicines
my blood was hard at work

it knew exactly how to make me better

thanks, mom

"I know the barriers and obstacles to feeling well must seem nearly insurmountable to you. We want to help you in any way that we can to find your way to wellness. That is our common goal. In the meanwhile, when people try to help you there, or ask about your well-being, meet them with kindness and patience. They have no way of knowing how difficult this is for you, and they may never know. Love them, despite how frustrating their actions are to you. Try to recognize when you are really frustrated with your situation, not them.

We are in this together, and we will always be there for you."

this is an excerpt from an e-mail from my mom
I am one lucky gal

Whoever you are, reading this: I hope that you have a support team that's stacked.

one of the first things
I wrote down

Health is no chemistry experiment
You can pop pills every 30 minutes and remain too sick to get
out of bed
So here's some things that it is:
It's a militant awareness of "let food be thy medicine" with every
single bite
It's a commitment to creativity and internal motivational speeches
to rival Olympic coaches
It's buying yourself flowers
It's moving as slowly as you need to while everyone swirls
around you
It's forgiving yourself for standing still while your peers are running
towards their goals
It's saying, "I am stronger than this" every morning into the mirror
It's sobbing in public, on floors, in your bed, on loved ones
It's panic attacks and counting to ten
It's using your sadness and anger to still find passion in life
It's knowing that most people will look at you and never know
It's knowing that even those who want to will never know
It's wondering how you will tell your partner one day about
this time
It's letting the fresh air knock you down for weeks until it starts
to feed you
It's laughing at the absurdest, most disgusting moments
It's lots of crying, did I mention crying?
It's making a pact with yourself to leave the house every day

It's taking sick days and breaking that rule to watch trashy movies in a blanket burrito
It's admitting when you're scared
It's getting comfortable with the unknown
It's saying thank you to God to the universe to the restaurant for the accommodation
It's an overwhelming sense of gratitude that brings you to your knees
It's forgiving yourself for not knowing sooner
It's hoping and knowing you will make a full recovery

RE/ made a solid point on Black Friday

I will not let this steal the ecstasy of lying in sunny grass
of throwing off my shoes and bounding across lumpy moss

I enjoy jumping off of waterfalls into chilly mountain pools
I adore stepping up mountainsides with determination

I will not hide inside
or constantly wear shoes
or pick the campsite with a worse view because the grass is mowed

we need to figure out how to cure this disease
the climate and our health care systems

and a good way to remember the magnitude of those tasks
is to play outside

remember your roots, and let them root for you

words fail when others ask what it feels like
but I've always been one for wacky metaphors
so I've started to tell them that my body is a tree

[because trees are great]

and for the past few years, I was so busy
with thick green leaves of youth, ambition, vitality
that I didn't see the wasps moving in and nesting

[wasps are also great [[pollinators]]]

each new tincture, herb, pharmaceutical
shakes my branches a little harder

the first shakes pissed off so many wasps that I was covered in stings
                    unrecognizable
and stuck horizontal, tending to my wounds

however, something that I am proud to remember
is that the branches never snapped
the trunk had more range of motion that I could've ever imagined

when I thought of yelling, "timber!"
my roots held strong

my sister held me on a street corner, with a firm but gentle mother's
tone while my breaths became fuller and more even
my roommate lay on her belly next to me on the dining room
wood, riding out a gust

they fed me

[because roots are really great]

to those of you who are sick

May your warm evenings sometimes become less paranoid
May you, one day, lie in a sunny patch of grass without fears

May we find a way to treat the larger disease
rather than attacking one symptom with chemicals sprayed to kill

May you walk with bare feet under the stars
May you float down a creek with your eyes gently shut

May we hear you when you're unable to do these things
and work harder to heal for the next orbit around the sun

to the tick

you shouldn't have bitten the back of my kneecap, fucker
in fact, it was your tragic flaw
you bit an artist
and I'm going to create and write and advocate
until everyone knows this story line

I don't wish you ill
pun intended
I hope my body swallowed your body with mercy

as you were absorbed into my skin
I hope it didn't hurt

after all, that bacteria rattled around dinosaurs' skulls before yours
it's not malicious
or delicious
it's just livin' its best life like the rest of us

I just got Cindy Lou Who'ed

I am an acrobat
every day
balancing the tightrope between pushing myself and allowing
rest that will heal

so in a stuffy hallway late last night
I told a dear friend,

"I can't tell if I want to go hiking tomorrow or if my Instagram
wants me to go hiking."

She is wise. She sent me off to bed with a hot tea and a question
to steep.

Will you enjoy it if you leave your phone at home? Will your
body thank you?

I am an acrobat. Arnold Schwarzenegger. I pick things up and
put them down.
I put down the need to be outside, proving my increasing vitality
to myself or anyone else.

my hope for you

I hope on days when you almost feel normal
except for the faint echo of a bug in your ear
or a tiny one trailing in your brain

when your belly almost feels strong

and your joints almost feel mobile

that you can forget
just for a minute

I hope you can forget forever one day
because I hope there will be a cure

sometimes random suffering points to not-so-random suffering

I cry when I see babies
Because I think of when my blood was clean
But then, who's to say that they were so lucky?
Who knows if the illnesses of the earth have given them the grace
of a healthy childhood

I was once mad at my parents for building their home on grass
crawling with ticks
I was mad at my parents' parents for spraying that grass with
chemicals from planes
I am grateful to my parents for building their home on the rolling
hills of my youth
I am sad for my parents that they have watched a child scream
in invisible desperation
I am eternally thankful that my parents believe me and helped
me find healing hands
I am choosing to move back to the fields near my parents
So that I can add their love to the medicines that I swallow, rub,
and breathe in

I traveled to a land of lumpy crossings
Breathing in the sea air
Seeping my tired muscles in sea water
Washing my traumatized, tear-stained cheeks with seaweed
Sat in a tomb-shaped stone and let it bring new life
Full of children's shrieks
Old folks' laughter

And the strong upper lips that line the cliffs where the Irish Sea meets the scraggly turf

Only the insecure try to eradicate every foreign object, making their land pure, virgin
The quiet, determined voices of wisdom are learning how to host hope
Keeping an even keel when immune systems flare up around them
Insisting "no surrender!"
Threatening to abandon the piper uppers who try something new

I'm learning that there is room within me for even this
As I lie spread wide in a bath, hearing the quickened thud of my pulse
Remembering what it was to float inside my ma
Connected directed towards the nutrients I was absorbing
Powerless to choose those exposures
As we all are

Neither did the gulf choose to wear a cloak of oil
Or the gales to wear down like a pebble in the toughest of torrents

I know what needs to be done
I need to lie face-first in that grass and hug the soil
Climb to the top of that dirt path and exchange forgiveness
With the beautifully broken creation that didn't mean to make us sick

so fresh so clean

if salt water is super restorative
then I can expect bright, young rings around my eyes
until I'm wrinkled like an apricot
because there have been tears soakin' into those skin cells on
the daily

thanks tears, I'm gonna pretend like you'll keep me young and
fabulous after all this

occupied

my medicine box is nearly empty
a doctor's appointment a short 2 weeks away
so why am I covered in a rash?
"I'll try to be a normal person who thinks nothing of this"
I think
as I walk into a work day
to find a man
HIV positive
who is talking about the challenges of that disease
the stigma of occupied blood
the hurtful encounters with members of the medical community

to the future members of a Lyme support network:
I'm going to fall into your embrace
so relieved to find you
relaxing into the time that is mine with people who understand
more fully
thank you for having the courage to walk through the door
I'll reward you by wrapping my arms around your torsos
like a non-crazy woman who has waited her turn

hiker praise

"I mean, you're not a serious hiker unless you have Lyme disease."

And for an instant
Juuuuust a second
I wore it like a badge of honor
Proud of the status and the googly eyes he was giving me

but that evaporated very quickly
like a crock of shit on a hot summer's day

riddle me this

Why oh why would I be able to sleep with these questions
bopping around my noggin?
Things like,
How did I have "no" symptoms for all of those years before
I started treatment?
Will the sensations ever go away?
Are they like tiny trolls that I've now successfully angered to the
point that they will forever attack my insides with tiny pickaxes
for retributive justice?
What are the freaking odds that a bug bite disease makes you
feel like there's bugs all up in your skin and brains?

Shhhhhh
count the sheeps
count to ten times ten times ten
go to sleep

press conference

Excuse me, miss? Listeners would love to know: What is your stance on biotics? They're all the rage and becoming increasingly common.

> "If it's during daylight hours, anti. I am firmly antibiotics. But closer to bed, and certainly if I'm doing an enema, I'd say pro! Probiotics all the way."

Do you think this will blow over?

> "Oh, definitely. I'd love to put biotics completely out of mind. And I do think that time will come."

sick of tears and skippin' the beers

Would I have chosen to take a few of my early twenties to be
completely sober?
HA
But, for now, while my brain is quick and nimble
I remember every dance party
every milestone celebration with the people I love
every seduction, flirtation, and getting-to-know-you chat
with crisp clarity
there is no hazy cloud over the memories of congratulations
late night conversations after a candlelit dinner
or hangovers or embarrassment from actions I am shocked
to have performed
scratch that
I am shocked that I found the confidence
and body positivity
to have more fun than the drinkers in the bar
I am shocked that I went streaking without a streak of liquor
in my blood
danced in a club without paying any money whatsoever
if I can do it, you can do it
and you don't need a chronic illness to accept that challenge

or don't and say you didn't because someone needs to drink all
of the delicious whiskey

British buddy

"Do you wanna get some beers? Oh . . . wait. No, you don't."
    "It's fine, I—"
"Fuckin' bugs."

And maybe it was his accent or the smile he wore as he cursed the entire insect kingdom, but I giggled and wanted to shower him in gifts. Thank you for the mischief in your eyes, buddy. Thank you for acknowledging that doom and gloom are a sometimes food like the diet-ridden cookie monster would say. I can't wait to hike, camp, and drink beers under the stars with you someday.

reframe

this one's for the girls who've ever had a ~~broken heart~~
                                        ~~chronic~~ illness
                                        resistant

I was resting, naked, after a hot shower
when my friend padded silently into the room
as tears rolled down my cheeks
I tried to swipe them away
muttering something like, "I want to be your fun friend, not the
girl who cries in bed all the time."
She climbed on top of the covers, interlaced our fingers, and met
my eyes
"Can you be both?"

a pox on the rutabaga!

when you look at a map and see the continents
does your brain travel to the man-made cities?
do you think of the attractions? the photos? the foods and delicacies?
when you think of the earth, do you think of the ways we have
planned for it to serve us?
I, for better or worse, have started to think first of the ways each
geographic chunk is suffering
as the temperatures change and the waves crash a little harder

when I think of Pennsylvania, I think of the warm winters and
the ticks who are surviving, thriving, and multiplying
less interested in undiscovered travel destinations
and more consumed by forgotten villages
the ones where floods are drowning farms

those changes, that's on us
we engineered the skylines
it's on you
it's on me
it's definitely not the fault of the rutabaga

I wonder how loud it would be if all of the insects
all of the mammals
all of the slithering, hopping, and soaring creatures
could yell their complaints for a minute

would something change if everyone was pissed about busted
eardrums?

a sidewalk somewhere

today, I went for a walk
and there were no more antibiotics in my stomach
just my cells
the tiniest powerhouses
leading me along
as every step felt like a testament to the ruggedness, tenderness,
and brilliance of the human body

maybe we're a destructive species
but when the destruction is funneled towards a disease
it's pretty incredible to behold

what if

Hi, how are you?
What's passing through you today?

Because you may not be well, but tomorrow will be different.
Maybe not better, but not stagnant.

How's your Lyme?
Are you actively squashing those spiro-shits?

So is Lymes something you have for life?
If this battle is long-term, I'm here for you. You're not alone.

I'll say it again. You're not alone.

apothecary banter

don't use water anymore to swallow pills
nope
gave up on that
'cause water is precious and stuff
and we gotta save the turtles and stuff

nah
I just let the capsules sit in my mouth for a bit
let the saliva do its thing
thicken, bathe the visitors and gulp them down

I like to call it saliva soup
nom, saliva soup, nommmmmmm

shots on shots

LAST NIGHT I DANCED MY FACE OFF
SWEATED
TOOK WATER SHOTS
WENT STREAKING AT 3AM ON GROUNDS WHERE THE
DALAI LAMA HAS WALKED
I POSED FOR PHOTOS AND LAUGHED AND TWERKED
ON WALLS
AND THEN I WOKE UP AND THOUGHT OOPS WAS I
SUPPOSED TO REST MORE
TOO BAD

I DARE YE TO PUSH YOURSELF INTO THE ZONE
THE FUN ZONE
BECAUSE FUCK BUGS YOU'RE A PARTY ANIMAL

take a break

How will I know when this book is done?
this isn't like any other experience of "sick" I've ever had
I can't just follow the doctor's orders and know that I'll get better

except I have

I've treated this thing like the world's longest flu
or the cold to end all colds

calmly swallowing the medicines and moving gently full
steam ahead

I may not know that the Lyme will fuck off
but I do know that I'll get better
I have gotten better

I've learned how the cells in my body respond to nighttime coos of
"You can do this. You're doing so well. You're beautiful."

Except for the moments when I'm not because spiro-shits are
taking center stage,
I'm the happiest I've ever been.

I'm better at seeing when something is unworthy of energy.
I'm better at looking behind behavior for other people's pains.
I'm better at putting words to feelings.
I'm better at boundaries and transparent self-care.

If you are reading this book, you may know all too well what
I'm talking about:

I don't want my loved ones to get sick, but I do want to give
them these gifts

the permission to walk out of a stressful situation and take a walk
or cry in a public bathroom
or write about their feelings with the confidence that someone
will care

In many ways, I'm grateful for this hell.
It has shown me the heaven I burn for.

heaven—an Earth free of disease
renewed by the humans who've forgotten how to garden

you lead, I'll follow

It's not about how sick you are

It's about what you're well enough to do

and if you heal your heart first

your body will follow

txts from last night

YOH

tried chromotherapy because why not right

strong pink is no joke

give it a try, but strong pink will mess you upppppp

in a good way

you know you've fallen deep into the health and wellness rabbit hole when you start talking about alternative medicine practices like they're your favorite cocktail

is it still a secret in a published book?

the things that connect us to everyone else
just a txt or a sentence to Siri away
are making us forget to connect with anyone else
and even
affecting the way that our cells connect with each other

but mention that to anyone else
and they won't want to talk to you anymore

so we'll keep it as our own little secret

my face amongst the trees

I'm no doctor, but I've started to secretly call myself a healer
because I know random things now
like how salt supports my adrenals

and the back of my Himalayan fancy salt says
that it was created 250 million years ago
during a time of pristine environmental integrity

and that makes me get really quiet
because people would sooner say that we have a purple sky
than that humans have fostered a time of pristine environmental
integrity
even though I believe we were designed to have symbiotic
relationships
with every moss and crab and elephant

so we need more people to start calling themselves healers
who look past one or two symptoms
to a larger, broken system
who become persistent caregivers
rather than prescribing powerful, quick fixes
and who pressure doctors to start doing the same
for our bodies
for our planet
for the recognition that they're joined

ran fresh outta words

how do you explain to someone that the intensity of this pain is
unlike anything you've ever experienced
or that you don't remember what it felt like before the pain a few
long months ago
you start saying things like
there's city sludge in my blood
and
my spleen is *not* havin' a good day
you don't recognize the person who's saying these things
but you find a way to be amused by her

splish-splash

have you ever walked a liiiiiiiittle too close to the curb on a city
sidewalk
when a bus came by
and gotten splashed head to toe with fuckin toxic shit that you
wanted nothing to do with
while you're on your way to do something really fun
and you think, "Well, I can't go now! What the hell?! Should I
end it all? Should I call an Uber?"
and then you question your life choices and think, "I shoulda
walked over THERE where all the smart, lucky people go!"
and then you lose all faith in yourself because you thought you
knew how to walk down a sidewalk, but it turns out, you can't
even do that without being a hazard to yourself
and then you blame the traffic systems at large
you think, "If people knew how to DRIVE, this wouldn't have
happened. A pox on that bus driver!"
so you recreate your transportation methods and become an
aggressive biker who won't go anywhere near buses at all?

No? Too specific?
Turns out, I was just painting a drawn-out metaphor for the
cycles of chronic illness that I have witnessed . . .
from fearing for your life
fighting for your life
losing interest in your life
and redefining your life

no, you didn't ask for this.
no, it isn't fair.
no, you're not an idiot for getting a tick bite.
yes, life will be beautiful again.

Tinder profile

if you try and date me,
I'm gonna have alllll kinds of new questions to ask you.

What do you do to balance your energy?
How would you describe your relationship with food?
How do you process change?
How does the description "people with poor health" sit with you?
When's the last time you played outside?

　　　　I guess that one's not new. It's just really important.

I do

I hate the word "chronic." I do.

Someone asked me the other day, "So is this something that's going to come back over and over on you?"

Like the bacteria are a boogeyman, waiting behind a bush, who will jump out and take me down at the exact wrong moments of my life

I blabbered something about how I've experienced the power of positive thinking

and I'm doing great, so that's where I'm focusing my attention

but then spent the day thinking, "How could that conversation have gone better? How can I explain this mental shift to the wonderful people in my life who are waiting for their genes to turn on them and ruin their stable comfort?"

I dunked a toe in the quantum physics and biology pool and boooooooy do I want to go swimming!

I'm beginning to understand how our cells are programmable, adaptable, and resilient.

I'm beginning to think about the pathways I've repetitively accessed when my body has outwardly signaled a response to temporary illness.

I've reached for pills.

I've looked to address the symptom so that it gets out of my way.

I'm beginning to understand just how much cells are affected by their environment.

I'm beginning to get frustrated with people who can't admit that they are walking, talking cells with no regard for cells with roots and tails.

For a long time after I was diagnosed with Lyme, I was scared to move about the world. I felt fragile. I was doing some very heavy internal lifting.

But this is what I'm beginning to hope:
this particular disease has made me think hard about the influence of the environment because it's a direct link
the tick bite made me sick
but the underlying lifestyle—this one that includes hiking, paddling, and seeing wonder in Nature's sexy curves
that lifestyle is what will continue to heal my cells
and as I've traveled to different corners and communities
I've seen how my infant country has polluted others and over-produced our way to sprawling, smog-choked swatches of space
While we imagine escaping to outer space when we're rich enough

That's what needs to change. And lucky us, those cells are built for change.

On a small scale, I'm not afraid to spend a night in a dusty B&B room.
The next day, I'll find a way to care for my cells with one of the millions of options from ancient healing practices.
And on a large scale, I'm not afraid to fight like hell for the cleanliness of our biosphere.
The next century, people and animals and plants and groupings of cells could exist without rampant disease, collapsing populations, or perpetual warfare.

I love the word "healing." I do.

road trip! where to?

once you realize that everyone is healing from something at any given moment
and you take the time to learn about how someone you love is healing
or even someone you just met who was courageous enough to talk about it
it will help you in your own walk towards wellness

"Hey, kid! Where ya goin?"
"The wellness well!"

accessible

If your former reality consisted of
walking or running around during the day
and lying down to sleep at night

And suddenly, walking, sleeping, even breathing is difficult
Life can be very frustrating

You may find yourself looking to people who've spent many days
with alternate realities
Those who've limped, scooted, or sat to pass the days
And learned to rest during darkness in their own way

They may help you find comfort
And you may never look away from these mentors
The ones who often stay erased from the currents of mainstream
attention

Welp.

Yesterday, I found myself in the sauna, thoughts blaring

"MWAHAHA melt!!! Die!!!! I'll outlive you alllllll!"

in a cartoonish, villainous voice

I was chortling at the absurdity
of defying tiny infections inside my skin as enemies that I could
video game destroy

      until I wasn't
              because maaaaajor yikes
              ice caps, dude
              and polar bears and stuff
              my words were a liiiiiiiiiiittle too real
for someone who claims to care more about cohabitation than
obliteration

Chekhovian delight

imagine a fluffy white towel in a pristine hotel room
or the deep intake of crisp air right before the tip of your kayak
totters over a rapid
the sensation of sunlight on your forehead
or the gentle lap of a retreating wave against your heel

those things
they're beautiful
because you've decided so

housekeeping could've worn the same gloves after cleaning the toilet
and a strainer could pull you under and trap you as the water
fills your lungs
exposure could give you cancer
and the water could be contaminated

the only difference is your perception

so, yes, I'll correct you when you tell me that I seem to be struggling
I will not put my nose up towards thinkers of hippie-dippie love

I will fill my body with light
love the tissues between my bones

say thank you to the people who loved me when I was young
who conditioned me to believe in belief

I'll do it all with a feeling of ease

House Keeping Team

lesson n°1: Dig,
dig,
dig,
dig,
dig,
dig!

lesson n°2:

Be a crab!

repetition

It's true
I don't know you

But I know of you
I know that your cells are negotiating within their community
your community
actively engaging in the peacemaking process that will result in
harmonious health

I know that you may be scared
I certainly was
But then I saw how impossible it was to heal while paralyzed by fear

I hope and I pray that you will begin to trust again

Maybe you'll find the hilarity of certain moments
or start meditating until you find serene lightness and joy

I don't know what your deal is, man
I just know that something made you pick up this book

So I also know that you have what it takes to say, "ok, today I
need to do what needs to be done."
Whether that means engaging in the spiritual practice of crying
or sticking probiotics up your butt

whatever it may be, you're not alone

banana peel

I may not be wholly healed
but I know that it's holy to heal
and at least I'm not a holey eel

Apostles of Beauty

Animals are impressionable
They have to be
I mean, if a log falls and crushes Uncle Stewey
It's helpful to remember stuff like that
So you don't end up like Stewey
Love you, man

Think of frogs
Pulling information through their skin
Contaminated or not
It will be absorbed and informative or lethal

Humans store those experiences too
Why would we not
Genetic makeups that are so similar to critters that it's something
like a miracle that we get to speak our thoughts out loud or type
them onto a screen with two twiddly thumbs
The difference, however
Is that we have yoga retreats

Science and techniques and ancient healing practices to clear and
move through that trauma
If you so please to use that word

Now, that's the responsibility we have
That doesn't lie upon the bullfrogs or sand fleas or sparrows
We know how to take pain and sin and transform it
So as to not transmit it

And there's one woman who comes to mind
Who has been battered
Her blood let
Her reproductive system
(The magic of the universe)
Maimed in an attempt to slow her spinning brilliance to the speed
that a man could wrap his lasso around
And hold in confident, calloused hands of authority
Her entrails are spilling from her abdomen
Hissing as her chi escapes
and she is gasping for breath

We could help her let go of her burdens
This sister earth of ours
That is
If we so choose

towards the end of a book, it's good to paraphrase

No, I do not believe that God made that tick bite me
That would be one fucked up agenda
If God infected over half of the staff of a summer church camp

Hey guys! You sang "Lord, prepare me to be a sanctuary," but
I like the chorus of "Days of Elijah" way better

Bullseyes on all of youuuu!!

No, I do not believe that God intended for this all along to shift
the trajectory of my life

Yes, I do believe that my belief in a God has helped me lean into
love during the toughest moments

No, I do not believe that you need to believe what I believe to
witness the power of belief

all for now

Horses
Dogs
They have a vaccine

It's natural for them to be outside
We've decided it's worth protecting them while they enjoy
the sunshine

But our children?
Nahhhh
We'll keep them indoors where it's safe
sheltered by the blue light of screens

It's not an epidemic if we just stay on the clean couch, right?

Acknowledgments

Katrine, Kat, & Kaitlin
I've never had so much fun surviving in my life

Mom & Dad
For believing me and loving me & always keeping me safe

My sisters
For staying patient as I've made my way back to you

The Wimberlys
For filling dark months with laughter, play, and newfound dreams

Seliner
Love you, wee fecker

Paola and Julianna
Thanks for giving me that fridge shelf, smelling so much salmon, and keeping a rubber chicken in plain view as inspo

Katie, Katie, Seanna, Alaina, and all of the fantastic practitioners at WholeHealth Chicago
For years of companioning me on this long, meandering journey towards a new normal

My fellow Corrymeelians
For doing life together during Catan but also the dreaded dishwasher discussions

Claire b, Elsa, Tamarah, Nikki, Jackie, Ally, Gracie, Abbi, Hardy, Julie, Annie, Brooke, Lauren, the cuddlefucker of Belfast and many more: Thank you.

a few years in the rearview

There are things I disagree with in these pages.
As I wrote them, they served a purpose.
They helped me laugh about how much I cry.

But I want you to know, dear reader, that I haven't
recovered to the body I knew before. I never will.
Each day in this little body can feel like a gift
and a battle. And it's a joy to live.

You can fight and rest and learn and heal.
You can. You've already started.

About the Author

Gail Tierney wrote *Not If, When* as a love letter to others with Lyme disease. She is currently attending grad school full time at Princeton Theological Seminary and also serving as Artistic Director of an eco-theatre troupe called The Kaleidoscapes. This one is for her granny—a warrior who showed her firsthand the extraordinary resilience of a survivor. She currently lives in Princeton, New Jersey.

Author photo © Alex Miller-Knaack

Selected Titles From She Writes Press

She Writes Press is an independent publishing company founded to serve women writers everywhere. Visit us at www.shewritespress.com.

Soul Psalms: Poems by U-Meleni Mhlaba-Adebo. $16.95, 978-1-63152-012-9. A powerful, lyrical collection of poetry that explores themes of identity, family, love, marriage, body image, and self-acceptance through the lens of a cross-cultural experience.

(R)evolution: The Girls Write Now 2016 Anthology by Girls Write Now. $19.95, 978-1-63152-083-9. The next installment in Girls Write Now's award-winning anthology series: a stunning collection of poetry and prose written by young women and their mentors in exploration of the theme of "Revolution."

Unfolding in Light: A Sisters' Journey in Photography and Poetry by Joan Scott and Claire Scott. $24.95, 978-1-63152-945-0. An elegant book of photographs, accompanied by poems, that invite readers to discover the beauty, simplicity, and spirituality that flows through hands.

Beautiful Affliction: A Memoir by Lene Fogelberg. $16.95, 978-1-63152-985-6. The true story of a young woman's struggle to raise a family while her body slowly deteriorates as the result of an undetected fatal heart disease.

Body 2.0: Finding My Edge Through Loss and Mastectomy by Krista Hammerbacher Haapala. An authentic, inspiring guide to reframing adversity that provides a new perspective on preventative mastectomy, told through the lens of the author's personal experience.

Painting Life: My Creative Journey Through Trauma by Carol K. Walsh. $16.95, 978-1-63152-099-0. Carol Walsh was a psychotherapist working with traumatized clients when she encountered her own traumatic experience; this is the story of how she used creativity and artistic expression to heal, recreate her life, and ultimately thrive.

9 781631 527357